The Fresh Fruit of the Spirit

Experiencing the Effortless Refreshment of God

by
Judi Manis

The Fresh Fruit of the Spirit
Experiencing the Effortless Refreshment of God

Copyright © 2018 by Judi Manis

ISBN: 978-1732529380

Empyrion Publishing
PO Box 784327
Winter Garden, FL
Info@EmpyrionPublishing.com

Unless otherwise noted, all Scripture quotations are from the New King James Version of the Bible.

NLT – New Living Translation
MSG – The Message

Dedicated to my amazing husband, Rick. You are proof that God is good and loves me personally. Thank you for encouraging me to dream big, for always believing in me, and for loving me so well.

Table of Contents

Love

As an apple tree produces apples without trying, so does Spirit produce after itself without effort. The fruit is a natural outpouring of what is flowing inside. Living by the Spirit (or living in the Kingdom of God) produces natural fruit. It's not something we can work on to get it to manifest. It's something that we inherit as a result of resting in our Father's love. Let's take a deeper look at the fresh fruit of love in regard to the first of the nine fruits of the Spirit.

In the Bible, we find a list of nine fruits of the Spirit described in Galatians 5 ~ love, joy, peace, patience, kindness, goodness, faithfulness, gentleness and self-control. Paul is encouraging the believers in Galatia to live according to their new nature. The very first fruit we see is LOVE. It blossoms out of us freely and naturally as we walk by the Spirit. My theory is that LOVE is listed as the first fruit of the Spirit because out of love comes all of the other fruit.

First be established in God's love for you

The fruit of love manifests out of us towards others only when we are established in our Father's all-encompassing love for us. His love is unconditional. His love is perfect. The Bible even defines God *as* love, meaning God has only good to offer us. It is a strong love, a compassionate love, a fierce love, a tender love. There are unending dimensions and facets to His love for us. Unlike human love, it is absolutely perfect. Without knowing our Father's love, without really trusting this, the fruit of love towards others does not flow freely through us out to the people around us.

Perhaps in the past we've heard that we need to fertilize and trim our trees so that the fruit will be more healthy and plentiful, but Jesus said, "I am the vine and my Father is the Gardener." The Gardener takes care of the fertilizing and the trimming of the dead branches. It is not for us to do this job. As we grow, we rest and trust our Father to care for us in this way. In the perspective of the natural man, trusting God's love doesn't make sense. It doesn't "work." It doesn't happen fast enough or with enough measurable rewards. Surely, we need to step in and "help" this process. Honestly, this kind of "help" usually ends up damaging what is growing.

The extent of His personal love

The extent of my Father's love for me can be seen in this: He formed me in my mother's womb and He knows me intimately. He knows that I tried to build a cabin out of rocks in the woods when I was child, so I could run away. He knows I tried to read all the women biographies in the Indiana County Library, that I love to make my husband laugh, that I am inspired by the arts, that I grew up on a farm and took care of the family pigs. He knows where I struggle and where I shine. He made my fingernails so that I rarely need a manicure, my eyebrows bushy, my legs long. He knows about the scar on my left knee when, as a kid, I fell on the ice walking down our lane.

These intricate details are his concern and they entail many aspects of who I am and why I am like I am. The beautiful thing is that He cares for all of these specific details. He even knows the exact number of hairs on my head. Only my Father, knowing all of these things, is in a position to love me best. He patiently takes into account all the various ways I have been made and impacted over time. He sees me, and He knows me, and He loves me. His love knows how best to approach me, how best to teach me, how best to feed me, how best to get my attention. His love is an ever-abounding source of gracious care for me.

Jesus looked on him and loved him

As I was considering the fruit of love, a passage of scripture came to mind which says that Jesus "looked on him and loved him". Such a tender reaction in the context. It's found in Mark 10:17-27 in the story of the rich young ruler. He was a Jewish leader in the synagogue. We know he was an upstanding leader, believing he had kept all the commandments from his youth. Clearly, he was vigilant and had made an effort to keep all the law. Yet, as happens with all of us when we try to keep the law by our own efforts, he still felt something was missing.

The rich young ruler asked Jesus, "What shall I do that I may inherit eternal life?" The rich young ruler wanted Jesus to tell him what more he needed to do so he could have the favor of God and inherit eternal life. This is how the natural world works. It makes sense in our minds and in our flesh that *we will try,* and *God will reward* our efforts.

Even though the man was claiming perfection with the law, Jesus knew this rich young ruler inside and out. He knew how hard he tried to follow all the laws of God. He understood the self-effort involved. He was aware of the wealth the young man had amassed, either from inheritance or from his position as a synagogue ruler. Jesus knew the man liked nice things, that he found his worth in his position. He knew the man could not possibly do what He was about to suggest. Yet before He responds, the passage says, "He looked on him and loved him." Such a beautiful and kind expression towards this man who was quagmired in a religious system.

Jesus takes the law to its furthest extent

Then Jesus said to him, "One thing you lack, go, sell whatever you have, and give to the poor, and you shall have treasure in heaven: and come, follow me." Jesus gives the expert commandment-keeper another command! He tells him to sell all he has and give it to the poor. This would then fulfill the extent of loving his neighbor as himself. He will have given EVERYTHING. Jesus also suggests that the rich young ruler give up his position in ministry and come, follow Him. Then the man will have fulfilled the full command of loving the Lord God with all his heart, soul and mind.

There, easy peasy, just do these two simple things and you will enter eternal life. The curious thing about Jesus is that He was often taking the law to its furthest extent, not just dealing with our outward actions, but our hearts' intentions, our thoughts, and inner motivations. Taking the law to its furthest extent ends only with perfection. Jesus was not trying to trick the rich young ruler. Rather, He was showing him the end of the path he was attempting to take. It is the path of self-effort. This is why we often feel like we've not done enough to please God. This is why we sometimes believe we've fallen short in our relationship with God. We were never meant to be able to carry out the law on our own. Even Jesus says this: "With men it is impossible, but not with God: for all things are possible with God." (Mark 10:27)

It is possible only with God

Only Jesus could give EVERYTHING. Only Jesus could fully fulfill every jot and tittle of the law. He was the only one capable. When we join with Him, we inherit all the blessings and provisions and promises of keeping the whole law (you can check out these promises in Deuteronomy 28). Jesus knew the rich young ruler couldn't do what He was suggesting, but He looked on him and loved him, knowing that He (Jesus) was about to go to the cross and do it for him. This is His extraordinary gift to the rich young ruler and to us, thoroughly gracious, completely undeserved, beautifully given. We are the recipients of His eternal love for us. In fact, this is the way it was meant to be from the beginning. In the Garden of Eden, we were *with* God. We relied on Him for our provision, our health, our satisfaction. It was a remarkable union.

Though it wasn't in our best interests to try and go it alone, we had the freedom to do so because love always gives freedom. It never controls. It was going to be hard for us as we tried to live disconnected from our Source. Yet God looked at us in our sad situation, sweating, full of fears, anxieties, meanness, even hatred towards Him, and He loved us. He loved us so much He gave everything He had, just so we could find our way back to our most fulfilling way of living: in union with Him.

Trying to keep the law without God causes your countenance to fall

When the rich young ruler realized he couldn't bring himself to give everything, his countenance fell, and he went away sorrowful. He wasn't going to inherit eternal life. Jesus looked around at his disciples and said, "How hard it is for those that have riches to enter into the Kingdom of God!" Why? Because natural man, disconnected from God and doing life on his own, finds it easier to trust in worldly riches than to trust in a God He doesn't know or trust.

Jesus' disciples were amazed at His words and said, "Then who can be saved?" In frustration, the disciples lifted their hands and asked, "If the standard is *that* high, who can possibly be saved?" It looks utterly impossible. This will always be the result when you try to accomplish the law on your own. You will walk away in sorrow and defeat, realizing you just don't have it in you to do all that the law requires. It will never be enough. But Jesus did fulfill ALL of the law and Jesus has given, for free, the gift of His Spirit so that you will never have to do life alone, never have to carry the burden of guilt and inferiority. You weren't made for that.

The fresh fruit of love

As you grow in your friendship and trust in God, and as you focus on His extraordinary love for you ~ the depths of it, the extent of it, the myriad of examples of it ~ you won't be able to help, ever so sweetly, to bear the fruit of love. You will experience the freshness of loving others who used to irritate you. The word 'love' has sometimes been translated as 'charity'. It is a gift freely given to someone who has not earned it and does not deserve it. That is the love God had for us *while we were yet sinners*. His love was not a reward for our good behavior. It was the precursor to our good behavior. It was a necessity for us to even be able to do anything good or truly be good.

Walking in the Spirit is as natural as breathing

Please don't be tempted to think that living by the Spirit is difficult. It's as natural as breathing. Like fish in the ocean and birds in the sky, it's actually how we operate best. Living outside of the Spirit is much harder, though most of us have been conditioned to think it is the normal way to live. Because of this, it may feel a bit unnatural at first, but give yourself grace to grow in it. Purpose to give attention to even the smallest evidences of fruit blossoming and growing in your life.

Jesus taught that whoever has, more will be given (see Mark 4:25). So, focus on the incredibly expansive love of God that you have been given. Don't just say, "Oh, I know God loves me. He loves everybody." Take time to really look at its beauty, ponder its dimensions, consider its clarity. As you look, listen, ponder, and consider these things, your heart becomes established in truth. The Father's love has the capacity to change your life, your health, your provision, your emotions, your future. And then, one day you will notice, as an apple blossom appears on a tree in Spring, a love that is beyond you has blossomed out of you towards someone you didn't have the strength to love before.

Look and see, the fresh fruit of love is growing in your heart, even as you read this!

Joy

Several years ago, I chose the word "joy" as something I wanted to work on in the coming year. I wasn't someone predisposed to positive thoughts and I desperately wanted to develop the quality of joy in my life. I was what you might call a natural melancholic. My thoughts and views tended more towards solemnity and negativity. That year, as I "worked on joy", I took a huge pay cut in my job, a relationship I really wanted to work out didn't, and I was asked by a friend I had been living with to move out. My life felt like one big struggle and, regardless of my sincerity, the year came and went without much joy.

My inner belief system was entrenched in disappointments, fears and frustrations, sprung out of my various outer circumstances that had built up over the years. I thought perhaps I was cursed, destined to never to be one of those lucky, joyous creatures I happened to know. "As a man thinks in his heart, so is he" (see Proverbs 23:7).

My feelings followed these thoughts, my inner beliefs. And because of this, my negative thoughts reinforced my negative feelings, which in turn fed my negative thoughts, and so on. You get the picture.

I didn't understand joy at all.

A fresh perspective of joy

In John 15:11, Jesus says, "These things have I spoken unto you, that my joy might remain in you, and that your joy might be full." Jesus had been talking about abiding in the vine so that our lives might bear fruit. One thing is clear: He wanted to be sure we had *His* joy. Though we know Jesus was familiar with suffering, He was also a joyful being. His first miracle was at a wedding party! He was even accused of being a wine-bibber and glutton by some. He wasn't, but He was so full of joy that they were suspicious of Him. Jesus also wanted us to have a joy that would *remain*, not come and go, or be dependent on anything temporary or shakable. This is joy without limit, a joy that is *full*, a joy that is alive.

Joy leaps and dances and bubbles up from the inside. It doesn't depend upon an outer situation or circumstance. Happiness, on the other hand, comes and goes, ever determined by who and what is around us. Joy, an unlimited celebration from within, is a result of knowing something life-giving. It can exist even amidst suffering and grief. It is un-diminishable, regardless of what is happening in the world around us. Joy is the blissful assurance that no matter what we are facing, we are not alone. We are deeply loved and cared for by the Source of all life.

The Kingdom of God is righteousness, peace and JOY

Jesus explained the Kingdom of God doesn't come by ocular observation but comes from within (see Luke 17:20-21). The Kingdom of God is even described in Romans 14:17 as "righteousness, peace and *joy* in the Holy Spirit" (*emphasis mine*). It stems out of what is inside us. If our inner belief is determined by a temporal and fallible human system, joy will be fleeting at best, especially at times of intense difficulties or pain. However, if our inner belief is firmly rooted in the eternal and reliable work of our loving Creator, we can rest assured that lasting joy will spring up with ease.

Joy is the natural byproduct of an eternal love. It is an inevitable fruit of the Holy Spirit living inside you. Joy happens naturally and without effort. It is there and, if you are aware of its presence, you can enjoy it anytime, day or night. When you know, deep down, that you are loved, you sense God's smile. You feel good, you feel safe, you feel a lovely sense of "all is well" regardless of the crazy natural life whirling around you.

And if you don't feel it right yet, you can know it first. Feelings will always follow your beliefs. So, start with what you are believing. Ground yourself in the truth of God's relentless love for you, His personal gift of His Kingdom to you, of His comforting presence with you... and the feelings of joy will inevitably blossom, its fragrance spreading over to your family and friends, your work, and even your challenges.

Joy is how you live best

It is very important that you know this: "It's the Father's good pleasure to *give* you the Kingdom" (see Luke 12:32, *emphasis mine*). What a delightful gift, utterly free and unearned! There is nothing you need to do but sink back into it. He wants you to live in it. You were made to thrive in its atmosphere. It's how you live best, the source of creativity, entrepreneurship, reconciliation, win-wins, unlimited abundance, and fulfillment. Your heart experiencing joy is His priority. Each morning, an emanating joy from an awareness of living in the Kingdom of God produces positive expectations for the coming day. Joy sees and expects the best in whatever situation comes up in the day.

Joy is the thrilling realization that the God who created the universe personally knows you and cares for you. It is the shocking realization that His forgiveness is thorough, your failures and shortcomings aren't being held against you! It's like owing $100,000,000 on your dream house only to find out the debt has been paid and you now own and can freely enjoy the whole estate. Joy also comes from the awareness that your Father handles your failures and shortcomings with care. He knows the whys and the wherefores and doesn't accuse or hurt you with shame and condemnation. Rather He understands and gently corrects. You feel safe and loved when He deals with them in you.

A quiet joy amidst the challenges of life

A few days ago, as Rick and I were leisurely walking after dinner through our neighborhood, I was aware of a quiet yet familiar sense of joy deep within me. I thought back over the day, remembering several things that had transpired which had the potential of ruining the day. We found out one of our cars, which has been in the shop now for two months, will take another two weeks before it will be ready. We also heard back from our homeowner's insurance company, after months of waiting, that we won't get any assistance with our deductible on our roof replacement. Yet these circumstances had no power to impact our inner joy. In fact, we had laughed, run errands, worked, ate our meals together, and had some great conversations.

There was a time when such news would have held me ransom to weary and overwhelmed feelings for an indefinite period of time. But the day had come and gone and neither of us had one negative thing to say. We experienced rest in the awareness of His loving care for us so we weren't living anxious.

Joy, an unlimited celebration within

What a change! What a wonderful gift to see it clearly that evening. The joy I felt, like the lovely afterglow of a close friend's dinner party, was a result of something bubbling up from inside me, a gift from Someone who adores me. That profound awareness of joy is like an anchor, holding me firm even amidst the storms of life. These days, I wake up and feel inner joy at simply being alive. The icing on the cake is that I also have food in my kitchen, a roof (with a few shingles missing) over my head. I hear the birds singing outside my window, our orange tree is bearing fruit in the back yard. Joy is just there.

If our bills are overdue, if we have a car that needs repaired, if we have some specific challenging situation, our joy is not diminished because there is this beautiful awareness of the presence of God, ever ready to walk us through it, give us creative ideas and solutions. He is with us, He cares for us and He wants to help us. How very fortunate we are to bear the fresh fruit of joy, a truly unlimited celebration from within.

Peace

Peace has always seemed a bit of an elusive concept to me, more of an ideal than an actual experience. I remember struggling with making an important decision several years ago and someone advising me "to follow peace" and I'd know what to do. That brought me such frustration because I didn't feel any peace about what the right decision was to make. I figured I'd get peace *after* I made the correct decision. I slogged through the anxiety and self-doubt, wrestling with the choices in front of me, consulting dozens of friends, mentors, really anyone who had an opinion, desperately (yet sincerely) trying to figure out which decision was best. The peace never came because, even after the decision was made, I continued to be concerned that I may have made the wrong choice.

In the natural, peace is the ever-elusive carrot on the stick... once I finish this goal, once I accomplish this task, once this negative circumstance is removed, once this issue is resolved, THEN I'll have peace. And if I ever got to the other side, I'd immediately find something else to "work on" (another goal, another task, another issue). I was never finished. You've probably heard the familiar sentiment, "There'll be time enough for peace when you're dead". This is the world's kind of peace: once you get healthy, once you fix this relationship, once you make this much money, once this circumstance is resolved... then you will experience peace.

Considering Jesus

But what if Jesus was for real? What if Him living, dying, arising from the dead, and sending the Holy Spirit, actually DID do something inside us? Maybe He did give us access to the Kingdom of Heaven (see Luke 12:32). Perhaps we really are new creations in Him (see 2 Corinthians 5:17). And maybe there is fruit within us, yearning to blossom outwardly without any help from us (see Galatians 5:22-23). If we take Him at His word, then all of this is not only possible, it's absolutely true!

Like love and joy, peace is your birthright as a believer. Once you believe, you are imparted with the whole kingdom, which includes peace and really everything you need for life and godliness (see 2 Peter 1:3). Regardless of what you may be seeing in the natural, the full inheritance is yours to receive, including all the gifts of the Spirit. They are not something you can control or make manifest. They are a natural outpouring of a Spring of Life inside you, bringing you supernatural strength and comfort and encouragement while walking through an imperfect world with imperfect people and situations.

The biblical words for peace

A portion of the Bible (the Old Testament) was written in Hebrew. The word for peace in the Hebrew language comes from the root "slm" or "shalom" which means "to be complete or to be sound". It has many nuances that include health, harmony between two parties, prosperity, success, fulfillment, as well as absence from war. It was used in greetings, both coming and going, and was considered a blessing to whoever you were encountering. Essentially you were saying to those you came into contact with, "May your life be filled with health, prosperity, and victory."

Another part of the Bible was written after Jesus died (the New Testament) in the Greek language. The New Testament has four primary sources (the gospels) which provide eye witness accounts of Jesus' life on earth, all of which confirm the miracles, the teaching, the healings, the death, burial and resurrection of the carpenter from Nazareth. The Greek word for peace was "eirene" which means "rest and tranquility," but often includes the nuances of the Hebrew word, "shalom". Jesus would have been familiar with and likely used both the Hebrew and Greek terms.

You've been given Jesus' peace

Before Jesus died, He had an encouraging conversation with his friends that we can read about in John 14. At one point, Jesus says to them, "Peace I leave with you, My peace I give to you; not as the world gives do I give you. Let not your heart be troubled, neither let it be afraid" (John 14:27). How does the world give peace? It is fleeting in coming and rarely lasting. Selfish people are at odds with each other every day because one wants one thing and the other wants another. It is simply the way of the natural flesh and it works from its own strength, sometimes able to overcome its selfishness, and sometimes not. But this is not the peace Jesus was referring to.

The disciples had seen firsthand the peace Jesus was talking about because they lived and traveled with Him. It hadn't come from overpowering anybody or bludgeoning them with truth or disrespecting anyone. It came from *inside* Him. He walked in peace, He spoke with peace and He even corrected in peace. They saw Him calm a raging storm! That peace inside of Him emanated out to utterly transform the physical wind and waves. They were in awe!

Peace: a treasure more valuable than money

Now He was preparing to leave them, and He was going to give them the gift of HIS peace. It's the very peace He walked around with. It was the peace that reigned in His heart when the Pharisees challenged Him, when they accused Him of being the devil, when His own family thought He was crazy, when He knew one of His best friends would betray Him. He had a treasure inside of Him that surpassed all the security that denarii or dollars attempt to provide in this world.

And He was GIVING it to them. Ultimately, Jesus would send His friends the Holy Spirit, so they could live and reign in peace for eternity, starting in the here and now.

An inevitable fruit that naturally blossoms out of the Holy Spirit is peace. It's not the kind of peace the world offers, the kind that is dependent on good circumstances or good behavior from those around you. It is a strong peace that sustains and strengthens you even in times of intense trials. Jesus told his disciples not to let their hearts be troubled and to not be afraid. Why? When we are troubled and in fear, we are operating from the world's natural system. He died for us to have something better. He wanted us to have peace, steadiness, assurance, calmness, rest. With the Holy Spirit this is not only possible, it is inevitable. We are better when we live in this manner rather than the other.

Normal natural feelings

It is completely normal for a human being to experience fear when he/she is in danger or facing something unknown that may potentially cause harm. It is normal for your flesh to feel anxiety if your circumstances are beyond your control. No one can fault you for natural feelings. You are a human being. Even Jesus, when He was in Gethsemane, felt these things, so much so that He was sweating drops of blood. Three times He went back to the Father. Three times He made sure this was the only way this gift could be given to us, and ultimately, He left the garden with peace and assurance in His heart, enough that He was able to face His captors, identify Himself for them, heal a soldier's ear and allow them to take Him to trial.

Some may think that the presence of peace then merely allows horrible things, does not confront wrong doing, or turns a blind eye to wrongs being done. This is not the case at all. But there can be a subtle temptation to act out of the flesh rather than the Spirit. This is something I learned very quickly when living as a missionary in rural Africa. There was so much sickness, disease, poverty, misinformation, hurts, it was truly overwhelming. Had I tried to confront and force a "fix" on the horrible things I saw in front of me, I would have burned out within a few months. There is a lot broken in this world and it was too much for me.

Being led

I learned to quietly pray and do what was impressed upon me by the Holy Spirit. If I was compelled in the natural I would become overwhelmed, stressed, self-pressured to make certain things happen, even helpful things. Nothing good or lasting came from that kind of energy. It only produced what I call "plastic fruit" (it looks good on the outside, but it doesn't provide any real nourishment). But when I was compelled in peace by the Holy Spirit to just listen or to make a meal, or teach a subject, there was an ease about it and life would spring forth. An undeniable effectiveness would ensue that was beyond me. This fruit was not only real, it was delicious. This confirmed in my heart that I was where I needed to be, doing exactly what needed to be done.

I certainly didn't always get this right, but gradually I learned to differentiate between flesh driven and Spirit inspired. There is a self-respect that acknowledges I cannot do everything I wish to change the world, even though I wholeheartedly want to. I don't get to override other people's free will, but I do have the Holy Spirit living in me. And if I go with Him, He will gently, ever so kindly, lead me to the next thing. There is so much more power and effectiveness in His way than in my flesh way. When I am in peace, it is easier to sense the Holy Spirit's leading. When I am in anxiety, it feels as if I am cut off. I'm not. God is always there, but my frustration, fear and anxiety have a way of giving the illusion that the channels are closed.

A real-life blossom of peace

Today, as I was driving to the grocery store, I found myself asking God what I could do to help in a current financial challenge I am facing. As I began listing off everything I was seeing in the natural, how it seemed to be getting worse not better, how I felt I wasn't working hard enough or contributing enough, I could feel the anxiety in me begin to manifest. Suddenly, I became aware that I was focused on *myself* ~ a burden *I* must carry, something *I* must do. Immediately, I switched to considering what *God* could do. I knew He did not want me stressed or anxious about finances. He wanted me to trust Him to provide. I didn't see the way or the how, but I know from experience He is my good, good Father. He will lead me forward.

There wasn't any big "Aha! I've got it all figured out now!" moment, but I did notice that the anxiety faded away and the lovely, now familiar peace, returned and I was free to go about my day with rest and thankfulness. The problem was still there, but I was no longer consumed with having to figure it out. I just had to put one foot in front of the other and go about my day with peace in my heart and mind. That peace puts me in a ready position, open and available to receive new ideas or possible solutions at any given moment. What happened today is just a small illustration of the lovely fruit of peace, peeking its head out in my daily life experience. More and more, peace is becoming my natural way of living. Trust me, it's a much better way to live!

Peace is yours for the receiving

Remember, you don't have to wait to see the outward manifestation of your solved problem before you have peace. In fact, the peace that is in you can have an impact on the circumstances around you. Simply be aware of the Truth (Jesus) within you. Our faith becomes effective by the acknowledging of every good thing which is in you in Christ (see Philemon 1:6). Peace is in you. Acknowledge it. Be thankful for it. Trust it. It is the fruit that comes from the Vine you are attached to.

Jesus says in John 16:33, "These things I have spoken to you, that in Me you may have peace. In the world you will have tribulation; but be of good cheer, I have overcome the world." Jesus clearly wanted us to have the better thing ~ peace ~ because His peace would have the ability to sustain us no matter what imperfect situation we'd find ourselves in. The fresh fruit of peace, more valuable than money, is ours for the receiving.

Patience

The fresh fruit of patience is exactly that: a fruit that grows out of an inside established in Truth. Patience is healthy. It's nourishing, both to you and to those around you. It is not difficult, and it is not something that comes from surviving difficult situations. In fact, you can endure numerous challenging trials and realize your patience is eroding rather than developing. Some believe God puts us through various situations in order to teach us to have certain qualities like patience. I think that is backwards. Jesus came to *give* us something we did not already have. He gave us the Holy Spirit (and as a result, all the fruit of the Spirit) to enable us to thrive and find fulfillment in this crazy, imperfect, and sometimes frustrating world. To do so, He knew we would need patience beyond ourselves.

Patience flows out of knowing the Truth about God's goodness and His unlimited love for you. If you believe things that aren't true, your ability to operate in patience will be limited. You will think you are threatened when others disagree with you. Frustration will be your normal. You will find that life is overwhelming you rather than you overcoming it. If, for example, you believe God is only happy with you when you behave well or have the right theology or the right politics, the patience you extend towards yourself and others will be limited in direct correlation to that belief. Truly, the supernatural fruit of patience can only grow out of an unlimited supply of God's love for you.

The superpower of patience

Patience is defined as "the capacity to accept or tolerate delay, trouble, or suffering without getting angry or upset". Wow! Can you imagine your world with the fullness of patience in it? It would be a world in which we enjoyed life, even in the midst of delays. Other drivers would be free to make mistakes (or even drive terribly) and you could happily wave them on. Facebook friends having different political and religious beliefs than you would be invited into your conversations and respectfully listened to. It'd be like possessing an awesome superpower! Everything from a slight inner irritation to a huge indignation would be overcome with patience.

This is exactly what Jesus gave us when He sent the Holy Spirit! He knew we would daily face delays, trouble, and suffering. He didn't want us to be living life continually angry or upset. It isn't good for our health, our relationships, or our quality of life. So, He offered us Himself which includes the supernatural quality of patience. Paul mentions that we glory in tribulations (see Romans 5:2) because this is the perfect opportunity for patience to do its work. In other words, we shine when we encounter challenges, because the world gets to see supernatural patience on display, and it is a beautiful sight to behold.

Why is it so hard?

Many people ask, "Why is it so hard to have patience?" If we try to be patient in and of ourselves, it is pretty near impossible. A single branch cannot produce fruit. However, if we are plugged into Life Himself, the impossible flows from Him through us. Without the fruit of patience, life is hard. Relationships are hard. Even trusting God can be hard. We trust more in our natural circumstances, what we see and feel and hear, than in God. It's easier. It seems to make sense. It's that way that *seems* right.

Like a piece of fruit, patience grows from the inside out. The sap in a vine makes its way to the end of a branch and appears as a tiny droplet in early spring. It then becomes a blossom. The blossom transforms into fruit. The fruit matures until it is ready for consumption. As you notice even the tiniest evidences of the fresh fruit of patience in your life, be sure to celebrate it. Don't get impatient with patience growing from the inside out. Let it take its time and the rewards will be beautiful, succulent and divine.

Long-suffering

Relationships are often damaged because of wrongs done, misunderstandings, differences of opinions. This can cause some of the most painful wounds in life. Sometimes this Greek word for patience is translated as *long-suffering*, which means "having or showing patience in spite of troubles, especially those caused by other people." Think of the inconveniences/hurts you've endured because of a spouse or child, of inconsiderate salespeople, co-workers or even friends. The fruit of patience is the perfect anecdote to overcome these troubles. Fruit grows, it matures, but it starts somewhere. And where it starts is with the Truth of your value and position in God. You are loved. You are forgiven. You are free.

Forbearance

Another word that patience can be defined as is *forbearance,* which means "patient self-control; restraint and tolerance; the action of refraining from exercising a legal right, especially enforcing the payment of a debt." Have you ever had a well-meaning friend say that "you have every right to be angry/frustrated/ upset"? Well, yes. I suppose I have a *right* to a negative feeling. But what does that profit me? I am left with an ugly, damaging emotion that is no good for me or anyone around me. Okay, I suppose I have a right to drink that poison, but it won't help me be healthy, it won't help my relationships to flourish, and it certainly won't help me to enjoy life.

Some may say it feels good to be angry, especially when you are in the right. I suppose it can feel good momentarily, but it ends up eroding your health, your ability to participate in loving relationships, and can push away the very things you need to experience a fulfilling life. Living in a sustained negative frame of mind is not the abundant life Jesus endured the Cross to secure for you. Some say, "Well, Jesus got mad in the temple, so I am justified in my anger." Jesus did not suddenly lose his temper in the temple. He was illustrating a point, not losing self-control.

Why do we need patience?

We share a planet with other people. Other people who are loved and adored by God, but perhaps don't know they are or refuse to believe they are. They look to their surroundings to prove whether God exists, rather than looking to God to help them navigate their surroundings well. We share our world with people who choose evil and people who make honest mistakes. We live with people who, because they are loved, are free, and unfortunately can use that freedom to cause harm.

I just had an argument with my husband. A silly one, but nevertheless a timely demonstration of the benefits of patience. Rick was telling me something about the car. I asked him a question. He answered me with what I perceived as irritation at my question. Immediately, I felt defensive and responded to him with irritation because he was irritated with me first. So where did we get? Two people experiencing the yucky feelings of irritation and defensiveness. Ugh! But what if I had paused for a moment before I had reacted? The fruit of patience could have done its work and we would both be experiencing our typical heaven-on-earth day. Still, the fact I am aware there are other options besides my reflexive emotions tells me that patience is growing within me.

Let patience do her work

"But let patience have its perfect work, that you may be perfect and complete, lacking nothing," (James 1:4). As you consider this verse, imagine *Patience* as a person. She is in the kitchen cooking a meal for you. It's healthy and delicious and she is doing all the work for you. Because you are not involved in the cooking process, you don't understand why it is taking so long. You become frustrated and even suspicious. You decide Patience isn't really working on your behalf, and because you don't trust her, you decide to kill her (when you don't let patience have its perfect work, you are basically killing her). Patience didn't get to finish her work and you didn't get to enjoy the nutritious meal she was preparing for you.

Patience is doing a work. It's not YOU doing the work to obtain patience. Patience is doing the work. All you have to do is let her. In season, you will taste the fruit of allowing Patience to do her work. If Jesus is in you, patience is there too. Your job is to let patience do her work on your behalf. Then you will receive the sweet reward of patience. It'll surprise you. Your emotional elasticity will extend even beyond what you thought possible. People will thank you for your patience with them and with situations that would normally drive others crazy.

Longing to see the sons of God

The reason other people are touched by this is because what they are actually seeing are Sons of God in action. The bible says creation is waiting eagerly to see such a thing (see Romans 8:19). They are longing to see the possibility of a supernatural (Spirit-led) life. It is breathtaking to see, just like watching an orchestra play a complex piece of music with precision and skill. Or witnessing an athlete accomplish a feat that defies physical limitations. Or seeing a doctor brilliantly use a new technique to do what has been never been done before. It's awe-inspiring. It is lovely to behold. It transports our hearts and spirit to the otherworldly, the eternal. Let's remember we are those Sons of God. We are in Christ and Christ is in us. The fresh fruit of patience is living and growing within us.

Kindness

The fresh fruit of kindness is a beautiful source of nourishment for a starving world rife with adversity, tribulations, and suffering. As with the fruit of love, joy, peace, and patience, this fruit grows out of a healthy life source. We see acts of kindness carried out among human beings regardless of their religious affiliation, and it is lovely to see. However, the spiritual fruit of kindness is beyond human kindness. It is above and beyond what we could think or imagine. It is something that arises within you just as gorgeous blossoms arise from a cherry tree in Spring, setting the world ablaze with its refreshing beauty. They can't help being gorgeous because their source is gorgeous. The outer reflects the inner.

The true vine

There is a reason Jesus claims to be the *true* vine (see John 15:1), and it isn't because He is rigidly intolerant or wants to preclude other ways to the

Father. It's because He is in the position to offer us the healthiest, most fulfilling way to live. He has taken the effort off of us and put it entirely on Himself, while every other manmade religion puts the effort back onto the individual. Jesus seems to reference that there are other vines we can attach ourselves to. Vines of self-effort, though they may produce some decent fruit at times, aren't the TRUE vine.

Just as birds were meant to fly and fish were meant to swim, Jesus wants for us to experience what we were made for: living in the unforced rhythms of grace. It is a much better way to live. Even with hardships or challenges that come from living in this world, He graciously offers us a way of dealing with those afflictions without stress and strain.

Paul's warning against mixture

There is also a reason why Paul adamantly warned the Galatians (and all his churches) against becoming ensnared in the works of the flesh, of turning to the old covenant of law to find peace with God. He tells them, "You have become estranged from Christ, you who attempt to be justified by law. You have fallen from grace," (see Galatians 5:4). Prior to that, he tells them that if they follow that route, "Christ will profit you nothing" (see Galatians 5:2). The teachers who were trying to persuade the church at Galatia were people who wanted to "help" them to do better, to improve, to be more like God. But, like the law, the self-effort involved would divide their attention, causing them to become unattached to the true vine, which is Jesus. Though tempting, it would actually prevent them from solely relying on Jesus.

It's the old "Tree of the Knowledge of Good and Evil" trick. Just take a bite so you can be better, be like God! Who wouldn't want to be more like God? He's awesome! It's just the wrong way to do it. It simply puts us on an endless treadmill of trying harder to grab the ever-elusive carrot on the stick. It brings stress, strain, wears us out and never really satisfies. Fully relying on Jesus is more like catching a wave on a surfboard, it carries you. It's a thrilling ride, because you become part of a bigger force than yourself.

"God's kindness leads us to repentance"
(Romans 2:4)

I've been thinking a lot lately about this verse. I know that some think fear of hell or divine retribution is what leads people to see their need for God. In fact, this was one of the motivating factors in my own life to go to an altar and recite a prayer after seeing a production displaying the horrors of an afterlife without God. It is also what motivated me to call my older brother on the phone, pleading with him to do the same so he would be safe and with me at the end of the world. (He politely refused to be entangled by my fear, regardless of my sincere beliefs.)

Unfortunately, this fear inside me also produced a proclivity to attach myself to the "right" group with the "right" beliefs that somehow elevated me above the "others" out there. It created a theology emanating from intellect and superiority rather than kindness and humility. Fear can drive us, just as under the Old Covenant I am sure that the fear of being stoned to death prevented some Jews from committing adultery, but it rarely produces an inner change.

Real inner change

The real change that Jesus was interested in, could never be attained by mere fear of punishment. If it had, Jesus could have simply joined the religious leaders of the day who handed out restrictions, rules and demands to be followed. This is what happens when "self" is involved: moral superiority cannot help but creep in, rigid demands on others cannot help but manifest, compassion is superseded by belonging to the "right" group. Jesus came to give us something altogether DIFFERENT. It wasn't based on the world system of control, fear, and lust. It was a spiritual system based on abundance, freedom and love. But how do you lead someone towards a different system when they have all their lives been conditioned to another? *Through kindness.*

"... that He might show the exceeding riches of His grace in His kindness toward us in Christ Jesus" (Ephesians 2:7)

This was evidenced in my own life. I was saved through a mixture of love and fear. I was definitely exposed to wonderful people and an idea of a loving God, but inside me, I wavered because I was never sure of what God was thinking. Was He the nice God who loved me or the angry God full of wrath who was ready, at any wrong turn, to smite me to dust and demolish my hopes for redemption? Was He a God with high expectations and when I didn't produce was angry at me or, at the very least, sadly disappointed in me?

As a result, not a whole lot changed on the inside of me. Oh, I tried harder. I read the Bible for hours, I worshipped for hours, tithed above and beyond the 10%, I volunteered, I fasted, I went to the mission field, I was willing to do whatever it took. No one could accuse me of not working hard, even in my relationship with God. And yet, I had an inner perception that I was producing nothing more than plastic fruit. It appeared good from the outside, but on the inside, I knew it was empty. It wasn't life. The fruit was coming from my own self-effort rather than the true vine.

Profound inner transformation

Fast forward a decade later. I began to hear and learn more about true Christianity, one that relied totally on Jesus, on His goodness, not on mine; on His strength, not on mine; on His grace and love. How could this be? I felt like I was experiencing "Opposite Day." I had always believed that resting or trusting in Jesus alone would bring complacency. And that was the LAST thing I wanted. I wanted to grow, to become better, to be more for God. I didn't want to sit on the bench and wait for God. That would lead to utter delusion. Or so I thought.

Instead, this is where the most profound inner transformation happened for me. God's kindness toward me led to my repentance. I wasn't repenting so much for immoral behavior. I was repenting for wrong thinking about God. So entrenched was I in fear of His wrath or His requirements of my perfect obedience, that I hadn't fully believed in His love for me. That He might actually *delight* in me, his darling adopted daughter. Could I really be the apple of His eye? Could He really love someone as imperfect as me?

God's kindness

As I sat quietly with Him, putting down all my good works FOR Him, I began to experience Him on a whole new level. And He was so very KIND. He was gentle with me, encouraging. It was as if He were holding my hand and taking me back to kindergarten where I could learn the most basic and elemental truth about Him ~ that He is love and that He loves me without conditions, no matter how badly or how good I behave.

Now if I behave badly and choose sin (and I certainly can), it will be to my own detriment. I will hurt myself or I will hurt others, and there often are ugly consequences to sin. However, avoidance of consequences was no longer my prime motivation to not sin. It was His kindness that attracted me towards Him. I saw that I was totally free in Christ. And yes, that freedom does open the door to choosing what is poison for me. But there is a beautiful place where you discover that Christ in you is stronger than any desire to operate out of the worldly flesh system. It is so much better to be in Him, to exude His life, His peace and kindness. It is truly the best way to live. I have no appetite for those old days and old ways. Complacency and self-effort were actually two sides of the same coin.

The fresh fruit of kindness

His kindness TRANSFORMED me on the inside! It did what the most regimented self-discipline of obedience never did, it turned a hard heart into a soft one. My heart became attached to His heart. My branch to His vine. His kindness towards me turned a girl who was extremely hard on herself (and therefore on other people) into a woman who enjoys being kind to herself (and therefore other people). "But when the kindness and love of God our Savior toward men appeared, not by works of righteousness which we have done, but according to His mercy He saved us..." (Titus 3:4-5)

A fruit of kindness appeared in my life. It was not me who produced it. In fact, it surprised me. I could feel myself growing, but it was a different kind of growth. More natural. More loving. With an awareness and ease in Christ. I no longer find that feeding on fear or offering it to others constitutes good news. What was the good news that actually had the power to bring inner change for me personally? It was, without doubt, an awareness of God's kindness towards me.

Goodness

The fresh fruit of goodness is evidence of the inherent character of God living in us. God is good. Goodness comes from God. In the beginning, as God created the earth with its grass, plants, flowers, and trees, He declared it "good." The same thing happened with the animals, birds, and fish. With each handiwork, He saw it and identified it as good. Out of goodness, He created what was good. Lastly, He created humans, male and female. Then God saw everything He had made, and indeed it was very good.

God was so good, He gave us the choice to either love Him back or not. He was brave and kind and generous. Our good Father wasn't interested in slaves. He made us to be like Him, in His image. He made us to be fruitful and to multiply. When we chose to disconnect from Him and go it alone, He knew it would be hard for us. However, that did not stop Him from being good to us. So good, in fact, that He came to earth to offer us a rescue from our own selfish, shortsightedness. He took our wrongs upon Himself and traded them for His perfect righteousness. He was good to us when, in our freedom, we least deserved it.

It is only goodness that gives extras

Recently, I came across a lovely quote by Sir Arthur Conan Doyle in his book, "The Naval Treaty" (The Memoirs of Sherlock Holmes). The main character notices a flower in the room and expresses: "What a lovely thing a rose is! ... Our highest assurance of the goodness of Providence seems to me to rest in flowers. All other things, our powers, our desires, our food, are all really necessary for our existence in the first instance. But this rose is an extra. Its smell and its color are an embellishment of life, not a condition of it. It is only goodness which gives extras, and so I say again that we have much to hope from the flowers."

I love this sentiment, not only because I love flowers, but because it beautifully describes the goodness of God. He provided *extras*: things we don't need but add remarkable beauty to our experience of life. Fish in the ocean are often brilliantly colorful, with striking designs, though they are rarely seen in the deep, dark waters.

Laughter! We are the only creatures possessing a sense of humor, the ability to communicate comedy and wit. Music, dance, art and theatre: these are wonderful expressions that elevate us above the mundane and inspire us to think outside the box. The sun could simply set each evening without its extraordinary display of colors and forms. These things are not requirements to living but are the above-and-beyond type of extras our God, in his pure goodness, is known for giving.

Beneficence

The Greek word for "goodness" is defined as an intrinsic quality and condition. It's not based on what we do, but rather who we are. Or rather, whose we are. Because God is good, and He created us in His likeness, and He rescued us from sin and death, we can choose to receive His goodness as our inheritance. Not merely human goodness, but divine goodness. Something benevolent and beneficial to those around us. We radiate a disposition that is kind, soft, winning and tender, mirroring our good Father. God's goodness goes beyond what is legally right, goes the extra mile, gives what is needed that will benefit, build up, and bless others.

The fruit of goodness is not the same thing we are seeking in self-improvement plans, whether they are religious or secular. There is certainly nothing wrong with self-help programs and life coaches as long as you are aware that often they are about making the flesh "good-er" rather than connecting to the true Source of life, where you operate from Someone Else's goodness. Of course, we want to become better at life and I am grateful for many of the courses and programs I've engaged in over the years. I've learned a lot from them, but none has provided the connection to God's life and goodness as in discovering the truth of what I've been given in Christ.

Untethered goodness

In Matthew 19:17, Jesus is speaking with the rich young ruler who asked Him what he must do to have eternal life. He calls Jesus "Good Teacher" and Jesus has an interesting response. He says, "Why do you call me good? No one is good but One, that is, God." He puts the focus back on God, not Himself. He calls the Father good.

The truth is that in the Garden of Eden, man chose to untether himself from God's goodness. It wasn't that they didn't have any "good" qualities by human standards, it was just that they no longer had *God's* goodness living in them. It wasn't until after the work of the Cross that we were able to be grafted back into God's goodness. Now it isn't merely human goodness that we possess, it is the indwelling of divine life.

Jesus graciously pointed the rich young ruler to the *Source* of goodness and eternal life. It doesn't come from following a set of rules or having high moral standards, though that is the best this world system offers. Even then, we can get stuck in dead works (just look at the Pharisees).

For godly life to happen, we must somehow be connected to the Source of all true life. That is why the Bible says that we were *dead* in sins. That eternal sap of goodness had dried up and, though we were physically alive, we weren't able to produce anything truly life-giving. We were stuck merely existing rather than divinely living, which is eternal life.

Goodness in action

In Acts 10:38, we are told that "Jesus went about doing good and healing all that were oppressed." He was generously benevolent to meet the needs of those around Him. He physically lightened their load. Jesus went about healing their diseases, so they could have productive lives. He cared for orphans and sinners and children and the mentally deranged. His Father's life-giving goodness was flowing through Him. Others could see it and were clearly drawn to Him. In fact, when you truly see the goodness of God, it is hard NOT to be drawn to Him.

In Matthew 12:35, Jesus says that "A good man out of the good treasure of his heart brings forth good things." A good man knows where his goodness comes from. Rather than claiming his own goodness, he knows that because he is attached to the Father, that beautiful quality of goodness flows through him.

I have a friend who is very beautiful, both inside and out. She is generous and optimistic and gracious. She is always looking for opportunities to help and bless others. Once I witnessed a lady giving her a huge compliment. She smiled and thanked her, but later when I brought it up, she simply winked and said, "That lady may not realize it, but it's Jesus she's really seeing." The compliment went to Jesus, and my friend was as thrilled as her admirer that she got to be a part of God's lavish goodness.

The fresh fruit of goodness

In the book of Romans, Paul not only assures the believers that they are full of goodness (see Romans 15:14) but he encourages them not to be overcome by evil, but rather overcome evil with good (see Romans 12:21). *Note that Paul is speaking after the cross, not before it.* Once you are joined with Christ, you are, by nature, filled with God's goodness. It is in you and can flow out of you in increasing measure. You have it and you grow in it.

Paul also gave them (and us) a vision of how the goodness of God would look in us (see Romans 12). He explained that we would look different from the normal human being. We'd have it in us to bless those who persecute us. When evil is done to us, we'd not repay it with evil. We'd have the ability to live peaceably with all men, not just those who agree with us. Our enemies would be fed by us, shown hospitality and mercy. This is a picture of the goodness of God towards the world.

Paul is not giving us rules to follow and then feel badly because we've come short. Rather, he's giving us a beautiful vision of how evil is conquered by good, so we can recognize it happening in our own lives.

I am aware that to do these things is not easy or simple, which is why most normal people cannot do it. We may not realize it, but we do have this ability in us and we can begin to express goodness to those who are unkind towards us, not in our human strength (that is impossible), but through Him who lives and breathes within us.

The "extras" of the Spirit

Goodness is a gift, an "extra" so to speak, just like love, joy, peace, patience and kindness. All are given as we connect with our Father. All are our birthright in Christ.

They are not given because we deserve them or worked hard for them. That would be payment, not a gift. They are not even given to us because they are necessary for our day-to-day survival. Rather, they are given to us by Someone who loves and adores us, because they are good for us, and because we are far better with them than without them.

As we acknowledge these beautiful gifts, we share the beauty of Christ's goodness with the world. These are our calling cards. These are our perfection within an imperfect world, within our own imperfect selves. My prayer is that all will see and believe! The view is gorgeous.

Faithfulness

The fresh fruit of faithfulness is a beautifully rich and confidence-building quality. I have titled this book about the fruit of the Spirit found in Galatians 5 "The Fresh Fruit of the Spirit". Why *fresh* fruit? Because for a long time I tried to "get" the fruit of the Spirit. I didn't see them manifesting as I would've liked, so I would "work" on them. This only produced what I experienced as *plastic* fruit. It looked good from the outside, but rarely offered any real refreshment to others or myself. Plastic fruit is empty, stale and impotent. Fresh fruit, on the other hand, is colorful, delicious, refreshing on a hot day, and full of nutrients. It is beautiful to see and satisfying to eat.

Those who try to work on or work up evidence of the fruit of the Spirit in their lives find that their knowledge about the fruit does not necessarily produce life. The fruit merely become a goal to shoot towards, to pray or hope for; an ideology or theory that, at best, is off somewhere in the future. This can be frustrating if you WANT to be a showcase of these lovely traits, but they don't seem to naturally bubble up. You may then feel compelled to WORK on them or BEG God to give them to you. Yet if we are truly *in Christ*, as the Bible clearly says every believer is, the full fruit of the Spirit is something we already have. It's fresh, it's life, it grows and matures in us, naturally and easily as we remember who and what we are as the *new creation*.

Jesus is the express image of the Father

To fully understand faithfulness, we must look at its origins. And for that we look directly at Jesus who was and is the express image of God (see Hebrews 1:1-3). By looking at Him, we can begin to catch a glimpse of what faithfulness is and what it looks like as it manifests in us. The Bible says that God is faithful even when we are not faithful (see 2 Timothy 2:13). And that He cannot *not* be faithful because He cannot deny Himself. The passage even says if we deny Him, He will deny us. As much as He adores us, if we choose to believe a lie, He cannot agree with us in that lie because He is the Truth. He gives freedom, which is essential for true love.

In Romans 5:8, we see that *"while we were yet sinners, He died for us."* If you really let that sink in, you realize that His faithfulness is independent of our good behavior or even our trying to be good. He was faithful regardless of us and our response to Him. When we sin, there are often serious consequences, but God is faithful despite us experiencing those consequences. The world was spiraling hopelessly toward self-destruction, yet Jesus came while we were down in the mud, slopping along. He did not wait until we got our act together before He gave His life for us. His gift was front-loaded. He gave us the gift before a guarantee could be given that we would even accept or respond to His amazing gift.

While we were yet sinners

Jesus was faithful to demonstrate to us the utter faithfulness of God. When we look at Jesus, we cannot help but see this facet of His enormous love for us that can be counted on no matter what we are going through or even how we are behaving. God's character of faithfulness cannot be changed or influenced by us. It is who He is. It is His nature to be faithful. To never give up on us. To be there for us no matter what craziness we've gotten ourselves into. His steadfastness means that He doesn't abandon us or become disappointed in us. He is committed to us in the extreme.

I remember going through a deep depression some years back. At the time, I even thought perhaps God had given up on me. But as I look back on that time in hindsight, I can clearly see how He was with me, gently encouraging me, sitting with me, comforting me. The depression wasn't magically or immediately taken away. It was manifesting because of some wrong beliefs I held as well as some consequences of poor choices I had made. I didn't know who I really was, so as much as I tried *not* to have depression, it reigned over me.

Jesus didn't have to agree with me to be there for me. He was kind and deliberate and patient as I began to absorb the truth that I had settled for something much less than His abundant life. It is touching to look back on such a painful time and see the faithfulness of a dear friend, refusing to give up or leave me in my despair.

The fresh fruit of faithfulness

Faithfulness is something that provides a sense of safety, security, builds confidence and a happy expectation of good. Because you know that the Creator of the Universe is for you, you are able to overcome, accomplish, or even endure anything. He will get you through whatever the current trial or tribulation. He will listen while you talk. He will encourage while you listen. He will understand. He will provide. He will inspire. He will accompany you as you walk through the valley. He will be your rescue. You can absolutely count on Him.

It is good to have the awareness that we are not always rescued *from* specific tribulations. Remember Jesus said that in this world we would have trials and tribulations (see John 16:33). However, we are rescued *through* specific tribulations. Jesus also said, "But take heart, I have overcome this world." This assures us that in Him we have overcome this world as well.

It is such an unbelievable good gift that He has given us a way into the Kingdom of God. This is not just for our future in heaven, but for our right now. When we can understand that this world is temporary and fading away, we see that His Kingdom is much more real than our natural one. It is a Kingdom of abundance and peace and strength rather than a kingdom based on lust, lack and pride. There is nothing better than resting in the now moment and enjoying the heaven all around. It is this experience of fullness and fulfillment in the present that is the anecdote for the lust of this world.

The faithful gardener

A seed of Christ has been planted in each of us. Our Father is a faithful gardener. I imagine Him excited and expectant as He tends to us while that seed takes root and begins to grow. We are often impatient to see the outcome of this seed in our natural lives, but God is patient, ever ready to adjust and water, or weed and fertilize. He is aware of the needs of each individual and is faithfully tending to us all the days of our lives.

My dad is a gardener. He has had a garden as long as I have known him. He never tires of growing things. In fact, the garden was a primary source of our family's sustenance for most of my growing up years. Now that it is just him and my mom living at home, he still gardens, giving most of his harvest to neighbors and friends. It is easy to see, that despite the work, he is quite happy to be in his garden.

I have taken note of a few things about gardeners. They stoop: they bend down to the precious plants they are caring for. They are tireless: whether for food or flowers, they endure the elements to be sure the plants mature. Patience is a quality they seem to possess: as the seasons change or as the needs of the plant change, they don't rush the growing process. They are consistent: day in and day out, they are there with their plants, caring and wanting good for their beloveds. I see the evidence of faithfulness in a good gardener that illustrates our dear Father's faithful love towards us.

A faithfulness that doesn't need

There is a whole book in the Old Testament (see Hosea) that illustrates the faithfulness of God with an unfaithful bride. With God's guidance, Hosea pursued the unfaithful Gomer. He didn't give up on her when most would. He understood her wounds. He cared for her amidst her own self-destruction. He loved her. He bore the pain of loving someone who refused to return that love. Somehow, a love that strong doesn't NEED the love to be returned. He just needed to give it and give it until it might possibly be received.

Faithfulness is a beautiful element of God's love. I see it reflected in my own marriage: in the eyes of my husband when he consistently and repeatedly speaks lovingly to me and reminds me that he sees me as beautiful. He does this even when I don't deserve it, when I am selfish or stubborn. He makes something ugly into something beautiful.

I have done the same for him. Once, when he had impatiently climbed down the baggage chute to try and rescue our lost luggage, the airport police ushered him into custody. I knew he had made the mistake without thinking and felt badly for it. Now I had a decision to make as to how I would handle the situation. I chose to tell him I loved him and that I would be waiting for him no matter what happened. It was a precious moment when I clearly saw that God had brought me into Rick's life to be there for him and love him whether things were going good or bad. The nature of my Father rose up in me and I was understanding, kind, and gracious. I knew that was how Rick would've been towards me if the situation had been reversed.

The source of our faithfulness

"But we all, with unveiled face, beholding as in a mirror the glory of the Lord, are being transformed into the same image from glory to glory, just as from the Lord, the Spirit." (2 Corinthians 3:18) As we look upon the tremendous faithfulness of God, we get a glimpse of what we ourselves possess as a believer. We see that we have it in us to remain faithful in challenging relationships, in difficult situations, with people and problems that tempt us to get rattled. It is something we are growing in. Yet it is unmistakably there, woven into our true selves.

Gentleness

What's so dynamic about *gentleness*? The word can, at times, conjure up images of passivity or being easily taken advantage of, or even impotency. This is far from the truth. The Greek word most often translated as "meekness" or "gentleness" means "gentle strength, which expresses power with reserve and gentleness". In other words, gentleness is extraordinary power that is tempered for love's sake.

God is gentle, but not without enormous power. Jesus demonstrated the gentleness of His Father in His day to day life on earth. When He died and rose again, He sent the promised Holy Spirit to gently minister to you and me. Because of the finished work of Christ, everything we will ever need has been given to us (see 2 Peter 1:3), and this includes the gift of gentleness. Simply put, the fresh fruit of gentleness is found inherently within the believer and it is activated by faith.

A person (even a believer) who does not know God to be gentle or who does not realize that gentleness was hers/his at the moment she/he believed in the finished work of Christ, will not operate in it outwardly. Her actions will be in accordance with her thoughts, her thoughts will follow her beliefs. A person who repeatedly reacts in frustration holds an inner belief that God is frustrated with her. Now, she may say she knows better, but in her heart of hearts, her actions are reflecting her true inner beliefs.

Have you ever noticed that a person with a propensity towards anger will read Jesus' words and see Jesus having anger and frustration, whereas someone without, can read the exact same words but see Jesus' kindness and caring instruction? What we believe (or have faith in) will ultimately be reflected in our own actions and behavior.

I am gentle and humble in heart

Jesus says in Matthew 11:23, "Take my yoke upon you and learn from Me, for *I am gentle* and humble in heart, and you will find rest for your souls" (*emphasis mine*). A yoke was meant to help the cattle work, not put them under stress and strain. A well-fitted yoke was a wonderful load-lifting provision. Jesus' yoke is likewise light and easy. Whenever you hear someone talking about how hard the Christian life is, take pause, because that is not what Jesus meant when He said He came to give us abundant life.

Life, in general, can be hard, but having the life of Jesus within us, learning from Him as He instructs, enables us to be at rest no matter what is happening around us. Please don't let this give you any sense of condemnation if you are experiencing a difficult time right now. Just know (and consider the fact) that He has provided for you the gentle strength to move forward. You have it now *and* you can grow in it.

Last week my Dad wrote to tell me that he and my brother had planted peas, beets, tomatoes and carrots in his garden. However, if you looked at his garden right now, you wouldn't see a thing. You might even be tempted to say that he doesn't have what he thinks he has. What he actually planted were *seeds*. Nevertheless, there are peas, beets, spinach and carrots forming as we read this. It's not even a matter of time and waiting for things to actually manifest. It's that, even *right now*, there are vegetables developing within his garden. Yes, they are growing, but *they also currently exist*. The same is true with gentleness. It is present within you and it is growing.

Walk in a worthy manner, with gentleness

"Walk in a manner worthy of the calling, with all humility and *gentleness*, with patience, showing tolerance for one another in love..." (Ephesians 4:1-2, *emphasis mine*). Paul is not giving the Ephesians a new law to follow, to inspire them/us to muster up the best part of ourselves to, in our human strength, be humble, gentle, patient and tolerant towards others. Have you ever tried it? Have you ever utterly failed? I have.

Human attributes, even good ones, tend to run out. There's an end to them. The fruit of the Spirit is endless. It is the love that *surpasses* knowledge. It is peace *beyond* our understanding. These fruits are not a part of the tree of the knowledge of good and evil. Even the good part of "good and evil" will fall short. Jesus took an ax to the root of that tree (see Luke 3:9). We don't try to be good and hope for the best; hope in the end that God grades on a curve. We drop our efforts, and graft into Him. We drop our filthy rags and we sink into the robe of righteousness.

Jesus said He came to give us life, and life abundantly (see John 15:15). Abundant life can, but does not necessarily, include material things or even situations that always go our way. Abundant life is living out of *His* eternal life rather than the knowledge of good and evil. When we live out of that first tree, we will become burdened, tired, stressed. We weren't meant to live that way. We were made for eternity. We were made to be recipients of the love of God, to have His protection, His provision, His care regardless of the outward circumstances.

Wisdom from above is gentle

It's funny how today so many people want to know where you stand on divisive issues. They demand that you strongly oppose those who don't believe "right". And rudeness is acceptable as long as the other person is in the "wrong." There is nothing further from the truth! God is gentle; it is His nature. When our faith clearly sees the finished work of Christ, we come alive on the inside. We begin to see the myriad of things that are included in that gift. Wisdom that is gentle and reasonable is a part of what we now possess. "But the wisdom from above is first pure, then peaceable, *gentle*, reasonable, full of mercy and good fruits, unwavering, without hypocrisy," (James 3:17, *emphasis mine*).

Did you ever notice how the Pharisees were often trying to get Jesus to take a stand in the knowledge of good and evil? "The Law of Moses says this, but what do you say?" (see John 8:5). Jesus would never partake of that tree. He always chose a third option: Life. His healing brought life. His teaching brought life. His death brought life. He was depositing the Tree of Life *inside* us. God so loved the world that He found a way to bring us back to the garden and access that tree of life. The tree of the knowledge of good and evil brought death. Even the good wears out, is fading away, is temporary. But the eternal is forever strong. It will last. It is the better way to live.

Gentle correction

"The Lord's bond-servant must not be quarrelsome, but be kind to all, able to teach, patient when wronged, *with gentleness correcting those who are in opposition,* if perhaps God may grant them repentance leading to the knowledge of the truth..." (2 Timothy 2:24-25, *emphasis mine*).

If you disagree with someone else's views, there is nothing wrong with sharing your opinion or correcting another's misinformation. However, how you do it will reveal whether you just want to feel better in the flesh or if you are aware of the larger eternal significance. Because if you are, the correction will be done in the spirit of God, not the spirit of hatred, disrespect or irritation. "Remind them to be subject to rulers, to authorities, to be obedient, to be ready for every good deed, to malign no one, to be peaceable, *gentle*, showing every consideration for all men" (Titus 3:1-2, *emphasis mine*).

A gentle answer turns away wrath

In Proverbs 15:1, we read "A gentle answer turns away wrath, but a harsh word stirs up anger." I love this scripture because it clearly depicts the strength and power of gentleness. The fresh fruit of gentleness actually has the ability to diffuse a potentially heated or harmful situation. This is how we differentiate human gentleness from the

Spirit-birthed gentleness. You become bigger than the person offering wrath. You are the bigger person when you offer gentleness rather than getting offended. It's as if you are outside the situation seeing the larger, eternal picture. You see what is truly important.

I realize this is an impossibility in the natural, but the spiritual gift planted in you gives you pause and the ability to offer something truly constructive. You don't *have to* use it, but you *can*. You just need to know it is there and is a lovely option available to you.

When you conduct yourself this way, you are actually operating in the "eternal" or from the Kingdom of Heaven. This is the Kingdom Jesus referred to when He said His Kingdom wasn't of this world (see John 18:36). His Kingdom is vast, expansive, powerful, and much more real than the Kingdom of this world. In fact, our worldly Kingdom was created out of His Kingdom. His Kingdom is eternal. It has no beginning and no end. It is outside of time. Our worldly Kingdom operates within and under His Kingdom.

Gentle Strength

I used to think strength came from confrontation, pointing out what's wrong, standing with the right people, holding firm to the good on the good and evil spectrum. It is the way that *seems* right (see Proverbs 14:12). But it isn't Life. It isn't being attached to the vine. All the fruit of the spirit blossom out of something much grander. They blossom out of God Himself. Living in you. Operating through you. Gently bringing nourishment to a dying world.

Self-Control

The fruit of self-control is easily misunderstood, and I've experienced the difference between carnal self-control and self-control that is a result of being grafted into the life of Christ. They are two very different narratives. One relies on self. The other relies on the Spirit.

I have often misunderstood the lack of immediate action on God's part as evidence that He was not interested or not involved so, therefore, I must take the reins and make what I deem necessary to happen, happen. If He doesn't do anything, I can't sit around waiting forever. It just doesn't seem right. God gave me a mind, right? Perhaps I was supposed to figure this out myself and bring it to pass using my own resources. Otherwise, I'd just feel like a passive observer and nothing would ever change.

Carnal self-control

What I've come to realize through personal experience is any change brought about this way is rarely lasting and definitely not fueled by LIFE. It is dead works. Though it is dead, it can appear to be good. But it is not alive with God's life. It's the difference between molding a plastic pear and a pear that appears naturally and effortlessly on a tree branch. Both can look good to a hungry soul, but the latter illustrates the way Christ has personally given us. A way that resonates with the very love and creativity of God.

In the past I have deeply admired men and women who seemed particularly strong in regard to self-control. They were what I saw as "successful" Christians. They rarely appeared to stumble and exhibited such ease and expertise with life (in comparison to me, Super Awkward Girl, constantly bumbling about). But truthfully, even "successful" flesh is still flesh. And flesh always produces death in some way or another. Now, I am not saying those I admired weren't led by the Spirit because I truly don't know their hearts (that is between them and God). But I was inspired and determined to get stronger in my flesh, so I could be like them. Surprisingly, I did become extremely self-disciplined in some areas, even to the point of being admired for it.

Of course, that pumped up my flesh, and made me feel much better about myself. After years of struggling, the results of this fleshly discipline became my "reward". After all, I had worked so hard. Now I could be an inspiration to others to work hard. The results were worth it, or so I thought. Arrogance and pride are death to the believer and that is what is eventually produced when trusting your own self-effort above the Holy Spirit. It was never my intention to become prideful or arrogant, but that feeling of just a wee bit of superiority over the next person was like a wildfire that rapidly spread through my heart. It wasn't healthy. And it wasn't life.

My testimony with food

One of the areas in which I have struggled with self-control has been with food. In the past, I have followed food plans, gone to self-help groups, engaged in counseling, and I've had varying degrees of success. However, a few years ago, I was enjoying life, especially after getting married. We were traveling and having a number of adventures. Life felt like one big celebration. Then I started noticing that I was eating when I wasn't hungry, and the weight wasn't coming off as easily as it had in the past. I was gaining weight and I didn't like how it felt. In fact, I physically didn't feel like myself.

One evening I sat down the on the couch with Rick while he was snacking on some pretzels. A determination came over me that I wouldn't have any pretzels. I wasn't hungry, and I didn't need them, and I just wasn't going to do it. Then, I found myself, without even realizing it, eating away at the very thing I didn't want. This was a breaking point for me. The worst part was not that I was eating pretzels. There is nothing wrong with snacking on pretzels. It was the feeling of not having control over my own body and desires.

Addiction and the Love of God

In the past, I have identified this as "addiction". Doing something I didn't want to do even when my intention was otherwise. In full disclosure, I have been treated for addictions in the past. However, this time, I was keenly aware that I wasn't believing right about something. My thoughts and beliefs weren't in line with my Father's.

I find that knowing the love and grace of God diminishes your appetite for control, self-condemnation, rigidity. They just don't go together. It doesn't feel natural. So, I knew the days of getting hard on myself, getting into a strict regimen weren't the answer for me. But I couldn't seem to get God to move to help me.

Then this thought: What if I already had everything I needed in Christ? That means the ability to treat my body with love and healthy self-care was inside me. All I needed to do was be aware. It started with placing my focus on the TRUTH. The truth that I am beautiful in my Father's eyes. That my body is beautiful to Him no matter the size or shape. The next thing was aligning my thoughts with His. Whenever I was tempted to get frustrated with the way my body looked or what the scale said, I would refute it and set my heart to agree with my loving Father. No one else (and nothing else) would determine my true identity. I was renewing my mind from entertaining lies to believing God's truth.

True identity

"Judi, your Father is pleased with you. Pleased with your looks. He will guide you to care for your body in a way that is loving and healthy."

"You have died with Christ, and He has set you free from the spiritual powers of this world. So why do you keep on following the rules of the world, such as, 'Don't handle! Don't taste! Don't touch!'? Such rules are mere human teachings about things that deteriorate as we use them. These rules may seem wise because they require strong devotion, pious self-denial, and severe bodily discipline. But they provide no help in conquering a person's evil desires." (Colossians 2:20-23 NLT)

If my desire was to overeat, whether it was for assuaging anxiety or for celebration or whatever, that desire was not more powerful than God's love for me. In fact, it was within an atmosphere of unconditional love that I could best make decisions to address this unhealthy desire. It was in such an atmosphere that I could grow and embrace optimal health.

Healthy changes

I hired a lovely online coach who taught me about healthy female specific diet and exercise in a way that resonated with me. I learned how my changing hormones were impacting my body as I aged. She guided me through my unique lifestyle challenges and helped me find what worked best for me. I don't have any rigid rules to follow and I haven't eliminated any particular food entirely, but I do tend to generally pick healthier things when I have the option. I am enjoying feeling healthy and young (probably the best I've felt in more than a decade). As a result, I've shed some of that weight, though I rarely weigh myself anymore. My favorite gift has been the ability to say the words, "No, thank you".

Trust me, I am far from perfect at this healthy lifestyle and I'm not exactly at what I used to call my "ideal weight" but much more importantly, I am learning to love my body just as it is, just as my Father does. Because of this, I am interested in treating it as best as I am able.

When I say life in the Spirit is effortless, I am not promoting laziness or doing nothing, as some may conclude. You will find the work you do is in a flow that comes easily and naturally. It's not without challenges, but somehow in conjunction with the Lord in you, it becomes fulfilling, enlightening, and fun. With the Lord's leading, we continually learn new things. We are flexible, experimenting and trying new things. You begin to recognize Spirit life/fruit in contrast with carnal self-control, which tends to bring with it a certain harshness. Jesus said, "For my yoke is easy and my burden light" (see Matthew 11:30). There is a yoke and there is a burden, but they are easy and light only because of the fact that we are joined with Him.

"Learn the unforced rhythms of grace. I won't lay anything heavy or ill-fitting on you. Keep company with me and you'll learn to live freely and lightly" (see Matthew 28-30, MSG).

The fresh fruit of self-control

I've often wondered why the word self-control uses that word "self" which gives the implication that all reliance is placed on the self. Not on something outside the self. The word in the Greek does mean "mastery, dominion within; proceeding out from within oneself, not by oneself." Clearly for the believer, this can only be accomplished by the power of the Lord who is residing within. We are a new creation in Christ. What we need resides within us in Him.

There are many areas of life that can be out of control in a person's life: finances, work, drugs, shopping, religion, sex, pleasing others, etc. Carnal self-control can seem tempting. It can seem reliable. But self-control that operates in death is never lasting. It eventually diminishes or morphs into another addiction. One of the best gifts of being in union with Christ has been the awareness that my flesh does not have control over me. Rather, the Spirit directs my flesh. Furthermore, this carnal world does not have ascendancy in my life. It is truly the unseen realm that is above and over my mortal reality.

Grace is the answer to ungodliness

"For the grace of God…teaches us to say 'No' to ungodliness and worldly passions, and to live self-controlled, upright and godly lives in this present age…" Isn't that wonderful? The goodness, the grace, the unmerited favor, the unconditional love of God (in fact, the same thing that provided us with salvation) is what overcomes ungodly and self-destructive habits. It is the very thing we initially supposed was too weak. Or wasn't enough. So, we built a system of religion, with additional rules, regulations, time tables, comparisons, confrontations, "helpful" templates to guide us towards what was already given to us. It was a system designed to "help" us but the true help comes from believing and receiving the empowering GRACE of God.

Just like love, joy, peace, patience, kindness, goodness, faithfulness, and gentleness, self-control is a beautiful fruit of the Spirit, evidence of divine life flowing in and through us. Each fruit is integrally bound to the others, complementing one another. They manifest first as a small bud and grow into a ripened delicious and nutritious fruit. This divine life flowing inside us allows us to become what we were always designed to be: loved, fully alive, living out our purpose of loving/transforming the world around us for good.

Author's Note

Dear reader, I hope you have enjoyed this book about the fresh fruit of the Spirit. Each individual fruit is yours in Christ Jesus. As you set your focus upon Him, may your awareness of His beautiful life inside you become palpable and distinctively real. The consciousness of this cannot help but be transformative.

My prayer is one of simple thanksgiving for hearts filled with love, joy, peace, patience, kindness, goodness, faithfulness, gentleness, and self-control. I also pray that each of you will grow in enjoyment of this LIFE we've been freely given. May you be blessed, as I have been, beyond your wildest imaginings. And may you know, without doubt, *how wide, how long, how high, and how deep his love is for you* (See Ephesians 3:16-20).

Connect with Judi online:

Blog: www.beautifulgracenotes.com
Website: www.rickmanis.com
Facebook: www.facebook.com/judi.hinson

About Judi Manis

Judi Manis has a BFA in theatre from the University of the Arts in Philadelphia. She has worked in various theater companies and shows at Walt Disney World. She taught theatre at a local high school and spent several years in Zambia, Africa, serving as a missionary. Since returning to the U.S. she has worked as an administrative assistant in business and ministry and has written a blog.

She currently accompanies her husband, Rick Manis, as he travels and ministers the good news of the gospel of God's unconditional love and grace for the world, sometimes joining him in teaching, counseling and encouraging.

She loves theatre, nature, domestic and international travel, reading, art, good conversations, entrepreneurship, hosting small dinner parties and simply being with friends and family. She is also the creator of "Noticing Heaven," a gratitude journal to record the good things in life.